Copyright © 2024 Cannabis Psychedelics Pty Ltd

Published by Cannabis Psychedelics Pty Ltd

www.cannabispsychedelics.com.au

All Rights Reserved. No part of this book may be reproduced by any mechanical, photographic, or electronic process, or in the form of a phonographic recording; nor may it be stored in a retrieval system, transmitted, or otherwise be copied for public or private use—other than for "fair use" as brief quotations embodied in articles and reviews—without prior written permission of the publisher.

The author of this book does not dispense medical advice and only offers information of a general nature for educational purposes. This book is not designed to take the place of advice from a qualified health professional, and there is no guarantee that the information presented in this book will be successful nor take into account the reader's circumstances.

Thus, neither the publisher nor the author assumes liability for any actions taken as a consequence of the information presented herein and any such liability is hereby expressly disclaimed.

The information herein has not been reviewed or approved by Government health authorities.

About the author

Paul Benhaim is one of the world's leading experts on cannabis sativa. He is the author of 9 books and 4 guides, as well as the founder of Cannabis Psychedelics. In the 20th Century, both the UK and in Australia Paul was responsible for the first hemp food companies. Pioneering the first hemp CBD businesses in Australia and Japan as well as building a $500m USA hemp company. Currently Paul is founder and chairman of The Hemp Plastic Company – a business built on producing plastics from this wonder plant.

Paul created the first company in Australia to look at legal production of psilocybin where he designed a clinical trial with a team of world experts.

Paul's first psychedelic experience was at the age of 17, and his journeys with many psychedelics have continued since then, inspiring his passions to work with nature. Having worked with the cannabis plant for three decades it was only recently that Paul recognised the ability for cannabis to be used as a true psychedelic.

An intentional Cannabis Psychedelic experience guided him to work with his global networks to share a well- considered protocol for healing based upon both science and ancient wisdom. This offering is now offered at his home through Cannabis Psychedelics. His direct spiritual connection with the cannabis plant has influenced the offer for legal cannabis users to meet and heal with this plant ally in a sacred, safe and intentional space.

Paul Benhaim

- The history of Cannabis as a Psychedelic, and why it has been used for thousands of years

- What cannabis is and how to know if the cannabis is good and gives you a psychedelic experience

- What is a psychedelic?

- Why we are built for cannabis – What is the endocannabinoid system

- How does cannabis differ from mushrooms and ayahuasca in a psychedelic experience

- Is this legal? Cannabis, psychedelics and the law

- Why should I have a cannabis psychedelic experience?

- If cannabis is dangerous, especially in a psychedelic experience

- What does a session look like? If you booked today, what is the process?

- Read some Testimonials. What others have gained from a cannabis psychedelic experience

- Psychedelic therapy is not cheap. What is the cost of Cannabis Psychedelics?

- Where to learn more

Cannabis is something I have worked with since I first was introduced to it recreationally (in the form of has) in the mid-1980s. My experiences took me to Thailand where I discovered 'weed'.

It was in the 1990s after I decided to make the first hemp food product in Europe that I went to my first High Times cup in Amsterdam. There I met with the likes of Jack Herer, Eagle Bill and Ben Dronkers (with whom I'm friends to this day). They taught me that smoking cannabis with tobacco was not the real experience and from that time on I learnt that this seemingly simple plant is more than what it seemed.

I focussed two decades of my career on promoting the nutritional and sustainable aspects of this amazing plant – pioneering the use of Hemp Foods in the UK, Europe and Australia, whilst in parallel developing the first commercial form of hemp plastic – for which I am still involved to this day. During this time I stayed predominantly away from the mind-altering part of the plant and focussed on psychology, marketing and business. At least professionally.

During my career I have written over 10 books (not including this short one), mentored others, set up manufacturing, and listed a public company on the ASX. One of my passion projects was founding a company called Delica whose focus is to manufacture psilocybin legally in Australia for the expected growth in the market. It was the focus on this 'magic mushroom' business that led me to re-look at the psychedelic explorations I had in the 80s and 90s in London, UK. I enjoyed discussing the uses of hemp at London nightclubs with the likes of Terrence McKenna and wonderful people such as Psycho Delic discussing the psychonauts' travels and poetry. These friends were the inspiration to look deeply into the inner world and the mirror it offers to not only ourselves, but to the future. It was in these deep experiences I realised that we are indeed all connected. Fast forward to 2022 and I discovered that Cannabis could not only be used as a true psychedelic but had been since history records began.

Despite enjoying 'the good life' living just outside of Byron Bay, in the sub-tropics of Australia, tending to a garden, swimming in a solar-powered chemical-free pool and using the techno tools and bio-hacking education for myself, I realised there was yet another project I had to share with the world – Cannabis Psychedelics.

In the next 2 years, I delved deep into my contacts file and asked around 30 of my friends from Europe, USA, Asia and throughout Australia to discuss specific aspects of the cannabis, psychedelic and cannabis psychedelic experience that they were experts in. This soon led to me creating a protocol for what I believe is the ultimate healing technology available today. And in this book, I will explain not only why, but what is included in this protocol I have been sharing with family, friends and now by word of mouth to the community. And all this is now completely legal in Australia.

May this practice lead to more respect for plants – who I believe are our equals, as is all of nature, including the animal kingdom of the sky, sea and land. May we experience the reverence and humbleness of being a small part in a much greater picture than we experience most days, whilst realising at the same time we are the universe having a human experience.

Paul

Cannabis is a plant. Some say a weed. It goes by many names in fact.

Cannabis is generally known as psychoactive (marijuana) or non-psychoactive (hemp). Both can be grown indoors or outdoors, and both contain hundreds of other chemicals – including cannabinoids, terpenes, esters and more.

There are broad leaf cannabis and narrow leaf cannabis. In the past people have called that Sativa or Indica, however, that is not correct as all the plants, like humans, are on a spectrum – something between Sativa and Indica.

NERD FACT:

THC is short for the cannabinoid Tetrahydrocannabinol (Δ^9-THC). This is the most common cannabinoid known for its psychoactive and psychedelic effects.

CBD is short for cannabinoid Cannabidiol – although psychoactive, you do not get the euphoric feeling of 'getting high' from this molecule.

Figure shows the structures of THC and CBD

THC

CBD

What is the endocannabinoid system?

The endocannabinoid system (ECS) is a biological system that regulates and controls many of our bodily functions, such as learning, memory, pain, inflammation, and appetite. It is composed of endocannabinoids, which are natural molecules that resemble those in the cannabis plant, and cannabinoid receptors, which are proteins that bind to endocannabinoids and cannabis molecules.

Humans are built for cannabis because we have an ECS that responds to the compounds in the plant, such as THC and CBD. These compounds can mimic or modulate the effects of our endocannabinoids, and thus influence our mood, cognition, immune system, and more. Humans can produce their cannabinoids. Mothers who breastfeed produce them in their milk.

NERD FACT:

Phytocannabinoids are found in plants while endocannabinoids are located within mammal bodies. The prefix "phyto" signifies that they are plant-derived in the former, while "endo" reveals the endogenous nature of the latter.

When we consume cannabis (eat, smoke, vape etc.) we use these **phyto**cannabinoids* to stimulate the cannabinoid receptors. Cannabinoid receptors are present throughout the body, but they are most densely packed in the brain. The **CB1 receptors*** are primarily found in the brain, but they are also present in the lungs, liver, and kidneys. The **CB2 receptors*** are mainly present in the immune system, in hematopoietic cells, and in parts of the brain.

EL SISTEMA ENDOCANNABINOIDE EN NUESTRO ORGANISMO

Los endocannabinoides (ECBs) junto con sus receptores (CB1R, CB2R) y los enzimas de su metabolismo, conforman un sistema ubicuo en nuestro cuerpo. Este sistema regula las funciones y sistemas principales del organismo y está destinado al mantenimiento de su homeostasis.

- 📍 ¿Dónde se expresa?
- ⚙ ¿Qué funciones cumple?
- ➕ ¿Qué patologías puede ayudarnos a tratar?

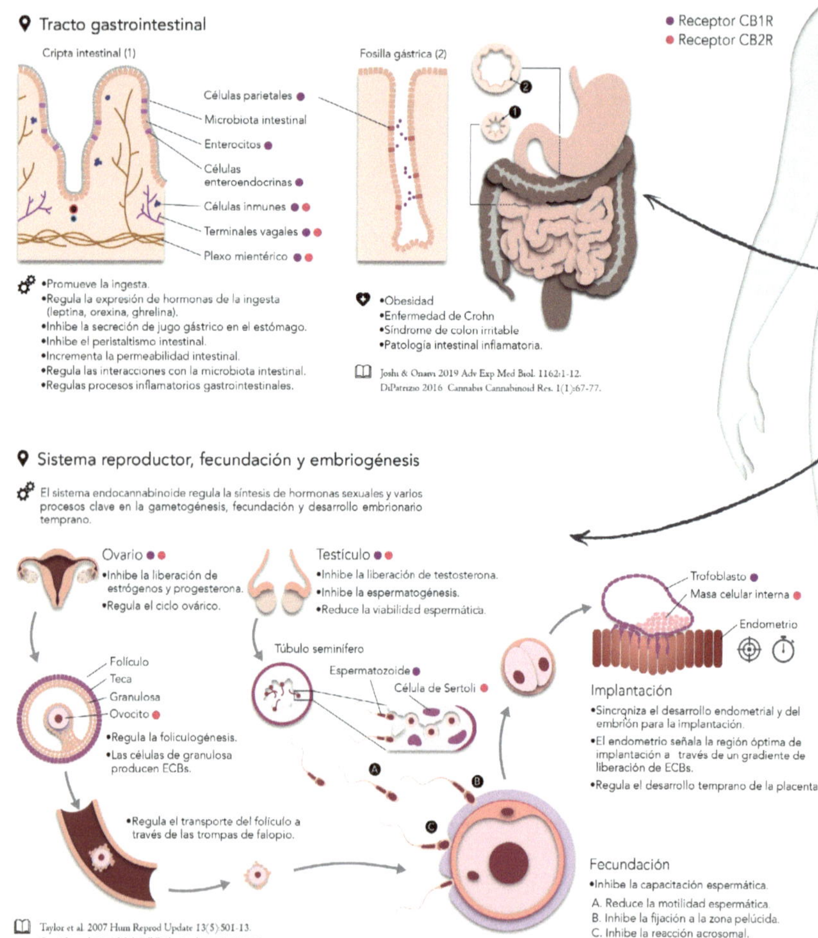

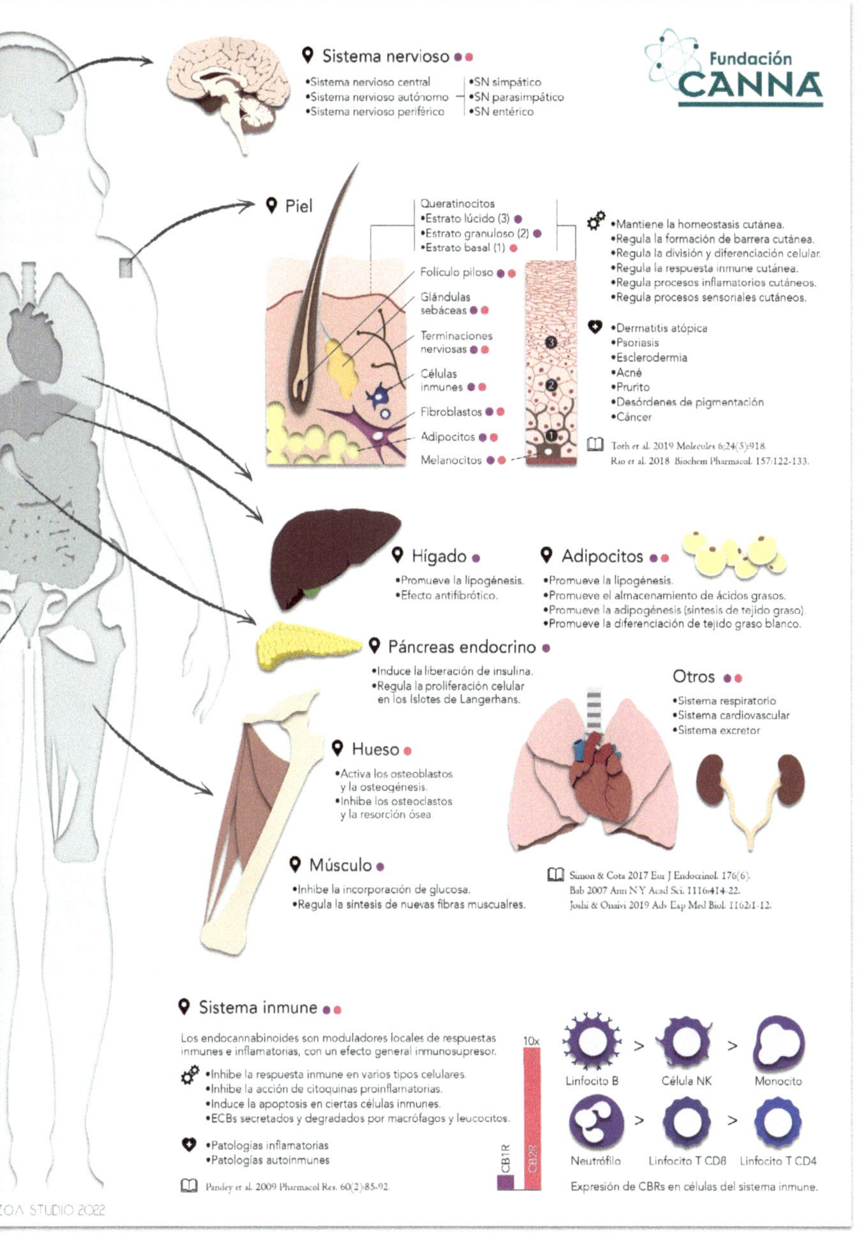

Fundación CANNA

Sistema nervioso
•Sistema nervioso central
•Sistema nervioso autónomo
•Sistema nervioso periférico
•SN simpático
•SN parasimpático
•SN entérico

Piel
Queratinocitos
•Estrato lúcido (3)
•Estrato granuloso (2)
•Estrato basal (1)
Folículo piloso
Glándulas sebáceas
Terminaciones nerviosas
Células inmunes
Fibroblastos
Adipocitos
Melanocitos

•Mantiene la homeostasis cutánea.
•Regula la formación de barrera cutánea.
•Regula la división y diferenciación celular.
•Regula la respuesta inmune cutánea.
•Regula procesos inflamatorios cutáneos.
•Regula procesos sensoriales cutáneos.

•Dermatitis atópica
•Psoriasis
•Esclerodermia
•Acné
•Prurito
•Desórdenes de pigmentación
•Cáncer

Toth et al. 2019 Molecules 6;24(5):918.
Rio et al. 2018 Biochem Pharmacol. 157:122-133.

Hígado
•Promueve la lipogénesis.
•Efecto antifibrótico.

Adipocitos
•Promueve la lipogénesis.
•Promueve el almacenamiento de ácidos grasos.
•Promueve la adipogénesis (síntesis de tejido graso).
•Promueve la diferenciación de tejido graso blanco.

Páncreas endocrino
•Induce la liberación de insulina.
•Regula la proliferación celular en los Islotes de Langerhans.

Otros
•Sistema respiratorio
•Sistema cardiovascular
•Sistema excretor

Hueso
•Activa los osteoblastos y la osteogénesis.
•Inhibe los osteoclastos y la resorción ósea.

Músculo
•Inhibe la incorporación de glucosa.
•Regula la síntesis de nuevas fibras muscualres.

Simon & Cota 2017 Eur J Endocrinol. 176(6).
Bab 2007 Ann N Y Acad Sci. 1116:414-22.
Joshi & Onaivi 2019 Adv Exp Med Biol. 1162:1-12.

Sistema inmune
Los endocannabinoides son moduladores locales de respuestas inmunes e inflamatorias, con un efecto general inmunosupresor.

•Inhibe la respuesta inmune en varios tipos celulares.
•Inhibe la acción de citoquinas proinflamatorias.
•Induce la apoptosis en ciertas células inmunes.
•ECBs secretados y degradados por macrófagos y leucocitos.

•Patologías inflamatorias
•Patologías autoinmunes

Pandey et al. 2009 Pharmacol Res. 60(2):85-92.

10x
CB1R
CB2R

Linfocito B   >   Célula NK   >   Monocito
Neutrófilo   >   Linfocito T CD8   >   Linfocito T CD4

Expresión de CBRs en células del sistema inmune.

ZOA STUDIO 2022

NERD FACT:

There are two well characterised cannabinoid receptors with distinct physiological properties. Both CB1 and CB2 are Class A G protein-coupled receptors (GPCRs). The CB1 receptor mediates most of the psychoactive effects of cannabinoids, whereas the CB2 receptor is principally involved in anti-inflammatory and immunosuppressive actions.

For a cannabis psychedelic experience, you will need cannabis with at least 15% delta 9 tetrahydrocannabinol – THC for short. The THC level does not determine the potency alone – what is known as the entourage effect does. The entourage effect is how the cannabinoids, terpenes, flavonoids, esters and other chemicals work together to produce an effect.

Cannabis, depending upon its constituents offers different effects – sometimes very heady, awakening and energising. Some bring you into your body, slow you down and help you sleep. It's not just the ingredients, but the method of consumption and particularly the dosage that affects your experience.

Today (early 2024) in Australia I see very little education about this subject as most recreational or medicinal consumers just want to get 'out of their mind' or have a mind-expanding experience. Most Doctors I have met prescribe cannabis based on its THC or CBD content. Some additionally prescribe based upon the predominant terpene content in balance with THC. I have yet to meet anyone teaching at the level we do in our Cannabis Psychedelic Facilitator course, where a friend from America who has spent 25 years on this very subject shares a scientific perspective with his wisdom.

The summary: smell the cannabis, if it smells good – that's where you begin. Ensure it does not have mould (not easy, requires tools), is fresh (when was it harvested/ cured/ packed?) and then try it. Start low, the smaller the dose the better – then work your way up. Write down how you feel (cannabis is often known for promoting forgetfulness). Repeat, and change dosages. Then decide if that variety is for you.

If it's from a good source it will have a Certificate of Analysis (CoA) that covers the full spectrum of ingredients – maybe the top 20-50.

You can then learn what the effect you felt from all of those chemicals means after you have tried several varieties. It doesn't get simpler – ie. when you have found a variety or two that offers you personally the desired effect you will want to know you can buy that again. The thing is, good quality cannabis starts degrading after just 3 months. 1 year old and I'd prefer not to consumer at all. So if you can get that same strain from the same grower, in the same conditions then

MAYBE it will have a similar effect. The truth is, if grown naturally each plant, and each harvest will be different – sometimes dramatically. Strain names mean very little. They do help with good starting genetics, but if you want the same effect you've simply got to try.

This is one of the main reasons I support legally growing your own medicine in your backyard – so you can control most of these factors as well as possible. And, in any case – don't worry as with our protocol, you can experience a cannabis psychedelic experience with almost any strain over 15% THC – it's just ideal if you follow the above.

If you have more than one strain – then mix them as you are more likely to get a wider range of cannabinoids, terpenes and other ingredients.

If you have low tolerance, then 0.2g may be enough to give you a deep psychedelic experience. If you do have a tolerance – then take a 1 – 3-day break (the more you consume, the longer break you should have) before you intend to have a cannabis psychedelic experience and go for at least 1g. Of course, you will have a legal prescription and you will follow the dosage guidance from your Doctor.

To put it in a (hempseed) nutshell, choose the freshest, naturally grown, all-round cannabis flower in its natural form. Know that the cannabis psychedelic experience is only partly determined by this and just as much, if not more by the well-designed protocol which includes: preparation, intention, set and setting, sound design, technology, aromatherapy, safety first and grounding tools. All of which are included in a professional cannabis psychedelic experience.

The word comes from the English "Psyche" or mind, and the Greek Delos or clear, manifest with the English addition of -ic the word Psychedelic or Mind Manifesting came about in the 1950s.

Merriam-Webster defines this as "of, relating to, or being drugs (such as LSD) capable of producing abnormal psychic effects (such as hallucinations) and sometimes psychotic states" and Oxord offers the definition of "relating to or denoting drugs (especially LSD) that produce hallucinations and apparent expansion of consciousness".

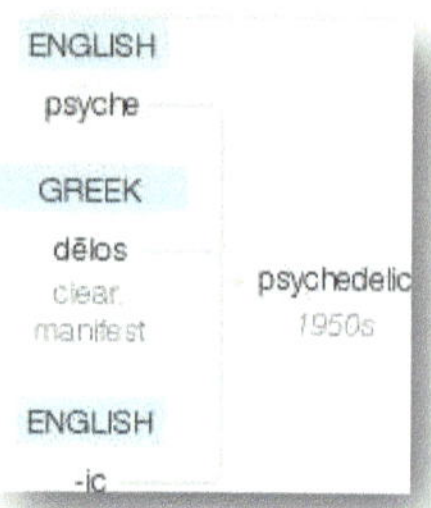

Get the picture?

Magic Mushrooms, or psilocybin or psilocin is a tryptamine substance that has been around as long as history records. Like its red and white cousin, Amanita Muscaria it is psychedelic.

MDMA is a synthetic drug developed in 1912. The more modern form, 3,4-Methylenedioxymethamphetamine (MDMA) is more of an empathogen-entactogen rather than a traditional psychedelic.

Ayahuasca was originally restricted to Peru, Brazil, Colombia and Ecuador until the middle 20th century when these vine leaves containing DMT, when mixed with a MAO inhibitor became popular for more widespread use as a tool for healing.

Cannabis, as described earlier is a plant that contains numerous ingredients of which THC is the known psychoactive compound (though there are many psychoactive compounds in cannabis).

There are many other psychoactive plants and medicines. DMT, mescaline, peyote, ketamine, ibogaine and more.

All the above-mentioned psychedelics can offer you a deep psychedelic experience – and all depend on the ideal set and setting. This includes the experience of your facilitator and the legality of the substance where you are taking it.

Cannabis, like DMT, ayahuasca and others can lead to vivid hallucinations, inwards travel to deep seated trauma and other experiences you may have forgotten or to an experience you had not considered that may not be directly related to your goal or intention, but EXACTLY what you need right now. So, in these terms —cannabis is a similar psychedelic substance to what is more commonly known as a psychedelic.

The main difference is that Cannabis is probably the MOST GENTLE of all psychedelics. So gentle that despite its ability to take you on a deep journey it is the only psychedelic where you have the agency to end the psychedelic experience at any time! If you have taken mushrooms or DMT – you know there is no 'turning it off' – you simply have to ride the wave of the experience, whatever that is like. Cannabis is not like that – she will gently guide you and if you choose – you can come back (albeit a little 'high'), ground and soon be back within the traditional world as we know it.

Most of these compounds are illegal for use, with exceptions predominantly being for traditional use in most places around the world. It is only recently that legalisation or decriminalisation has happened. Eg, Psilocybin is now federally legal in Australia and can now be used in Colorado, USA. Cannabis is now federally legal in Thailand, many states of the USA and now throughout Australia.

Focussing on Australia – Cannabis is legal to grow and possess or use in small amounts in the Australian Capital Territory (ACT) including Canberra. It is not legal but decriminalised. The rest of Australia made cannabis completely legal in 2016, but only for medical use.

To obtain cannabis legally you must ask a Doctor for this product. If you have tried something else that has failed and the Doctor deems it helpful and suitable you may receive a prescription for a particular form of cannabis – possibly flower or oil (edible or vape). Be sure to know what is available to ensure you get the best quality product you can that is fresh, supplied with a CoA and preferably grown organically. The prescription will allow you to access your product through a Chemist run by a qualified Pharmacist. This maybe online (where they will send you the medicine) or from a cannabis specific dispensary, or from your local pharmacy (who will likely have to order the product in).

The use of psilocybin and MDMA are also legal in Australia since 2023 for medical use – the first country in the world to do so. Though, as you will learn in the next chapter – they are not readily accessible.

Cannabis is apparently prescribed or used for various reasons that may include pain, anxiety, sleep or other specific symptoms. The people I have spoken to use cannabis to improve their feelings of self- worth, improve resiliency to anxiety, reduce their self-doubt, and increase their confidence, positivity, and motivation.

If you are ready to unlock the healing potential inside yourself and want to use your prescription for cannabis respectfully, and appropriately and gain the most out of it – then we recommend you book a cannabis psychedelic experience now.

Don't just believe us, read what others have said about their experience:

"I am a psychotherapist interested in the healing potentials of psychoactive plants. I recently experienced a psychedelic cannabis session. My experiences with other psychedelics have been powerful and insightful, but often harsh on my nervous system and physical body. I had some preconceived ideas about cannabis and associated it with feeling stoned and spacey. This was nothing like that, it was clear and vibrant with visuals that guided me through my intentions. I had agency to keep in certain visuals or move out as needed. This therapeutic psychedelic is something I think could have great value for many mental health diagnoses but also for anyone wanting to take a deeper look into their inner world" - Charlotte B.

"Paul facilitates a powerful experience for profound transformation. His years of experience with this master plant are evident in the way he confidently holds the space and guides you through each step of the process. I experienced some strong

shifts in my body and mind as I went through the process and came out feeling grounded and relaxed. His aftercare is gentle and present, I can tell he's very passionate about this work. I highly recommend Paul." - Edward L.

"How lucky I feel to have had the opportunity to sit in ceremony with Paul. I found such safety in this experience, as I was given detailed information before the journey and in the ceremony. My personal history made me a little frightened before sitting, as my mind loves to control. I was comforted throughout and had a really beautiful experience. I received

insights and understandings for myself. I must also say that the musical journey was sensational! I would recommend this to all that feel called." - Casey B.

"Paul was very professional, kind and balanced in his guidance of this journey. I would recommend it when one is wanting a safe and yet powerful experience." - Masih G.

"I found the Cannabis Psychedelic Journey quite restorative and healing. It was a gentle yet highly effective experience. I had a deep connection to my body and could feel how it held what I no longer needed. Since the journey, I have felt a sense of peace, openness and expansiveness. It was very gentle on my nervous system, and I

developed a newfound openness. " - Samantha Psychotherapist.

"Wow! Life changing. I did not expect such an experience with cannabis. This clearly intentional process allowed me to journey within myself in a supported and safe way. This is a new way to use my cannabis medicine that no doctor has ever shared. Highly recommend." - Jane F

"My psychedelic journey provided me with such deep healing. I found I was able to shine the light on some of my shadows, to face my fears, to look at deep seated trauma still in my body, and to become aware of some unconscious patterns that were playing out in my life. I walked away from the experience feeling empowered, strong, brave, lighter, and with a deeper sense of trust in myself, others and life at large. I am so grateful for Paul's space holding, and to this wonderful plant medicine." - Eva S.

"I am an experienced and regular cannabis smoker and never expected this. Wow, what an incredible journey! This psychedelic cannabis experience took me on an internal adventure like no other. The vibrant colors and enhanced sensory perception made me feel like I was exploring a whole new drug.

It sparked some deep introspection and left me with a new level of creativity and a profound sense of connection to others in my life. Truly an unforgettable and enlightening experience! I would even love to try it with the cannabis one day as the experience is so well put together - well done Paul. That soundtrack is amazing" - Richard G

Well, the experience has started – by reading this book you are arming yourself with good knowledge of this good medicine.

Step 1 - Learn

Once you have gained all the information you need from here, and the videos and Frequently Asked Questions and you have chosen if you want an in person, group or the ideal one on one VIP experience – you just have to <u>Book Now at www.cannabispsychedelics.com.au</u>.

Step 2 – Book and complete your medical intake

You will then pay your $37 deposit, choose a date for your experience and receive your medical intake forms. You can fill these out immediately online. Please do so as truthfully as possible as all the information within is highly confidential and for your benefit. It will allow your facilitator to get to know you more.

Step 3 – Your consultation

You will receive confirmation for a time/ day to speak with your facilitator. Usually on Zoom or equivalent. On this day you will have the opportunity to ask any burning questions and your facilitator will do the same – this will last until you are both clear and willing to proceed.

If there are any issues at this stage then you may still get a 100% refund. If you do choose to proceed then the time for your experience will be confirmed, including what to expect. You will be left with instructions on how to create your goals and intentions and what to bring for the experience. Simply comfy clothes, a water bottle, your preferred snacks (we supply some) and anything else you want to be comfortable. Oh, and your cannabis.

Step 4 – The experience

Your experience will vary in person, group or VIP – let me explain the one-on-one experience at Paul's retreat home above Byron Bay. For this you will arrive at the pre-arranged time, say 1 pm. You will be introduced to the space and set up the post-experience snacks, drinks and any objects you prefer.

You will be talked through the process before you move into the actual cannabis psychedelic experience – part 1.

This begins with preparing your medication and the preferred form of imbibing. We recommend the best German vaporiser for this. We then go through a simple, non-denominational ritual giving our respect and intentions to the spirit of the cannabis plant and you will have the opportunity to take the appropriate dose for you (we will lead you carefully and closely through this process). You will then lay down – in the VIP experience on our multi-sensory technodelic sound bed. You will be offered an eye mask, or our light machine (depending upon your experience).

After being guided through one or more meditations your well designed sound experience will take you on a journey, where you go in this journey depends on your openness, ability to be mindful, intentions and past experiences. Don't worry – no experience is necessary – we will guide you wherever you are at.

Cannabis is the MOST gentle of all psychedelics and offers one thing no other psychedelic can offer – the ability to leave the psychedelic experience. So, around halfway we will give you this opportunity and suggest you take a bathroom break, before having another opportunity to imbibe more medicine and begin another sound journey led in and out of with specific meditations just for you.

At any point of the journey you will have the agency to ask for more medicine, have a break or anything else you may choose. However, we recommend laying still and observing the internal experience and what this brings. We may enhance the experience through vibration, light or aromatherapy designed for you.

At the end, we will gently lead you out of the experience and into journaling. We encourage little talking until you have had plenty of time to write, draw, or take note of your experience.

From there we will lead you through specific and simple grounding exercises to bring you back. This may include all of your senses.

You will have pre-arranged a friend to collect you, a stay overnight or Uber as it is not legal to drive on cannabis and we want to ensure you get home safely. Most people sleep like a baby.

We recommend you take the rest of the day/evening slowly. Ideally, the following day, be extra mindful of any feelings or emotions that may arise and add them immediately to your journal. Within a few days, you will have already arranged a follow up call and that is when we de-brief. At no point do we force or ask you to share your personal intentions/ goals or anything else you prefer to keep to yourself. Though you are welcome to share if that helps you. We will discuss the process and ongoing integration of your experience which is usually deeper and more profound than most people expect from the most gentle of psychedelics.

And then the rest of your life begins!

The group experience is usually similar, especially when it is a small group that consists of you and a close friend, family member, partner or co-founder. And even if you choose a public group session, it is clearly stated that whatever happens is confidential and especially.

anything that happens to anyone else is not to be discussed outside of the session or integration. In group sessions, there is a group integration and an opportunity to extend to a personalised integration session.

At any point in the above journey, you will have the opportunity to bring along your psychotherapist or find a trusted plant medicine (cannabis psychedelic experienced) professional to continue supporting you. We can recommend such people on request.

I hope that explains what the actual experience will be like for you. Please know that behind the scenes we do a lot to ensure your safety, security and the smoothest ride possible by using ancient wisdom blended with modern techniques and technologies.

Together we can elevate beyond the high and expand our consciousness for deep transformation to become the person we truly are inside.

Problems. What to do when something goes 'wrong'?

Well, let me start here with the fact that, if you have followed the protocol in our Cannabis Psychedelic Facilitator Training Course then the chances of something going wrong are close to none.

Cannabis is scientifically speaking physiologically safer than water. Yup, you read that write. Though there are some common things we will go through that may lead to 'challenges, see below, it is worth considering the meaning of 'right' and 'wrong'. Ie. Have you ever had some challenges in your life that seemed 'wrong' when later, in retrospect they were learning experiences that supported your growth? I suggest we consider that in this conversation. And this conversation is far from complete – ie. this is in no way any medical guidance, or recommendation to consume cannabis or try this by yourself. In all psychedelic experiences, it is highly recommended to have a considered, experienced and focused guide. That is why we created the Cannabis Psychedelic Facilitators training course, where we cover contraindications with a clinical pharmacist, we discuss challenges from a psychiatrist's perspective and how to deal with things in the moment from various psychotherapy lenses.

Remembering that this is a simple introduction, and yet I wanted to touch on a few things:

- **Tight chest or heart-beat increase** – yes, this is common and real with consumption of cannabis and other psychedelics, and *usually,* this is nothing to worry about. If you have any history of heart problems then you should certainly speak with your Doctor about this first or choose a guide who is qualified to care for you in any circumstance where this is a problem. In my career of working with many people who have tried large amounts of cannabis and had challenges with their 'heartbeat' – it has always been in their mind. I don't mean to belittle the experience as sometimes it feels 'real'. The feeling is usually created by the psychedelics' ability to change the perception of time and other senses. So, when there is a lack of another stimulus the focus can be on your bodily functions.

It is good to remember that the heart beats by itself and does not require any help to do this. And that hearing your heart for the first time, or feeling it speed up or slow down can create anxious feelings. When I experience this, and I still do with some varieties of cannabis that I try, then the first thing I do is to remind myself that no one has ever died directly from cannabis. This is quite an astounding fact that pretty much always calms my nervous system. Focusing on the music or breathing and remembering mindfulness practices always helps here too.

- **Chest pain** can be something a lot more serious, which is why all Cannabis Psychedelic Facilitators are first aid and CPR trained to deal with anything. If you are unsure – always call an ambulance first. Chances are you will feel silly in the morning, but that's better than not acting if it wasn't the cannabis, but something else.

- **Previous negative experiences with cannabis.** Usually from edibles, usually at high school – this is a frequent experience and some people never try cannabis again, until they meet us. Cannabis Psychedelic Facilitators are here to re-introduce you to the spirit of the plant in a gentle way, in a new way that recognises the power of the plant. Especially if you have had a negative experience in the past, yet have experience or are aware of the benefits of medical cannabis and want to try again – then you are definitely in the right place!

- **"I felt uncomfortable in my surroundings".** This is the 'setting' part that is so crucial in all psychedelic experiences. We do not recommend consuming cannabis in public until you are very experienced unless you are feeling very safe and comfortable in your environment. The safest environment is a controlled environment with someone who is experienced and aware of what you are going through.

- **"I get stuck in my mind".** This is the 'set' or 'mindset' part of the experience and the reason I have written intention and goal setting exercises. Maybe they seem pointless, hippy or not like you, please be aware there is a lot of science and reasoning behind this part of the process which you can learn more about in the Cannabis Psychedelic Facilitator training course.

- **Cottonmouth.** Does your mouth feel dry? This is a common condition and is usually a sign you are not hydrated enough – drink a couple of glasses of water. In our cannabis psychedelic experiences, we always have water and sugar-free gum around to suck on or chew. This stimulates saliva production which may combat the feeling of dry mouth. If this happens often, consider limiting your caffeine content, washing your mouth with an alcohol free mouthwash designed to combat dry mouth will help. Repeat as you need. Don't forget oral health, which starts with a healthy lifestyle.

Any or all of the above can be seen as experiences. Coming back to the is this right or wrong, let's use the example of cottonmouth. Cottonmouth is not fun, and it doesn't feel 'right'. We have some choices:

1) Believe it's just wrong and do nothing, be in pain.

2) Deal with the immediate symptoms, drink some water and eat a candy and feel empowered that you did something.

3) Do 2) and then journal about it – why did this happen to me? Do I take care of my oral hygiene enough? Do I drink enough water? Do I eat enough healthy foods? What is the cannabis planting telling me that I can improve and journal about in the long term? Integration is the action that you take from these lessons or 'problems'.

When Australia legalised Psilocybin and MDMA my friends and I celebrated. When we read the fine print we realised it was not going to be easily accessible. After 6 months of legalising these two psychedelics, I believe only one person (out of 26 million) has accessed them. Why? I believe not just the large amount of paperwork – but the cost. On average my psychiatrist friend suggests $20-30,000 would be the out-of-pocket cost. Not many can afford that, and those that can are more likely to go underground – kind of defeating the purpose of legalising?

Cannabis Psychedelics was born to make this far more accessible – no more than AU$1,000 for a private session, including medical intake forms and interview, 4 hours in person experience, grounding and a subsequent integration session. This can be extended of course depending upon one's needs. The cost can be reduced further if you choose an online group session – less than $250.

You can learn to become a cannabis psychedelic facilitator for $3,950 – which is phenomenal value if you compare it with other psychedelic courses (especially in Australia) that lead to no practical outcome.

Check out all of our programs here:

https://cannabispsychedelics.com.au/programs/

We are focused on supporting the healing of others through intentional and safe settings for deep transformational experiences through the use of cannabis sativa.

To further enhance your understanding and connect with a community of like-minded individuals, we invite you to visit our dedicated platform: www.cannabispsychedelics.com.au. Here, you'll find a wealth of resources, community forums, and expert insights to support you on your journey.

Our Facebook page is https://www.facebook.com/THCpsychedelics- please like and share.

Our platform is designed to foster mindful connections, provide up-to-date information, and create a space for open dialogue about the responsible use of cannabis psychedelics. Join our community of seekers, explorers, and visionaries as we continue to share knowledge, experiences, and collective wisdom.

Enjoy our FAQ – full of lots of information about our experiences.
https://cannabispsychedelics.com.au/faq/
Enjoy learning about our Programs – learn about our private, group and online opportunities, as well as our weeklong immersion in Thailand, or the Nine Perfect Strangers retreat!
https://cannabispsychedelics.com.au/programs/

Facilitator Training – maybe this is for you? Just email us for a course curriculum: connect@cannabispsychedelics.com.au .

41

Remember, the journey with cannabis psychedelics is a unique and personal adventure. With mindfulness as your guide, you have the opportunity to unlock profound insights, nurture personal growth, and contribute to a community that values shared learning.

Embark on this transformative path with intentionality, and may your exploration of cannabis psychedelics be filled with mindfulness, connection, and a deeper understanding of the inner landscapes that await you.

Oh, and if you haven't yet entered – do make sure you have registered to win a free VIP experience for you or a loved one – all you need to do is share the email of the person you want to win here:

https://cannabispsychedelics.com.au/competition/

Paul and the team at Cannabis Psychedelics.